OF GRAVITY & ANGELS

For Julia Winiarski —
In gratitude for your warm
support of the marriage of
words and wine —

Jan Hirshfield

ALSO BY JANE HIRSHFIELD

Poetry

Alaya

The October Palace

Translation
(with Mariko Aratani)

The Ink Dark Moon:
Love Poems by Ono no Komachi and Izumi
Shikibu, Women of the Ancient Japanese Court

WESLEYAN POETRY

OF GRAVITY & ANGELS

JANE HIRSHFIELD

WESLEYAN UNIVERSITY PRESS

For Michael

WESLEYAN UNIVERSITY PRESS
Published by University Press of New England,
Hanover, NH 03755

Printed in the United States of America   10   9   8   7   6

CIP data appear at the end of the book.

The author wishes to thank the John Simon Guggenheim Memorial Foundation, the San Francisco Foundation, and Yaddo for their general assistance during the writing of this book.

The following poems appeared first in these magazines:
"Ars Poetica," "At Night," "Completing the Weave," "Dialogue," "For What Binds Us," "Heat," "Invocation," "Osiris," "See How the Roads Are Strewn," and "That Falling" in *The American Poetry Review;* "The Song" in *The Atlantic;* "Lullabye" in *The Georgia Review;* "November, Remembering Voltaire" in *The New Yorker;* "To Hear the Falling World" and "Evening, Late Fall" in *The Paris Review.*

Other poems were first published in:
Amicus, The Antioch Review, Black Warrior Review, The California Quarterly, The Christian Science Monitor, Crosscurrents, Ironwood, The Marin Review, New Letters, The Ontario Review, Pinchpenny, Poetry Flash, Poetry Now, The San Diego Poets Press Anthology, The Sonora Review, The Suisan Valley Review, Tellus, Yellow Silk, and *Zyzzyva.* "Justice Without Passion" appeared in the 1988 *Pushcart Prize Anthology.*

CONTENTS

1. TO HEAR THE FALLING WORLD

2. FOR WHAT BINDS US

3. THE OTHER EARTH

4. THE PATTERN THAT CONNECTS

1

TO HEAR THE FALLING WORLD

AFTER WORK

I stop the car along the pasture edge,
gather up bags of corncobs from the back,
and get out.
Two whistles, one for each,
and familiar sounds draw close in darkness—
cadence of hoof on hardened bottomland,
twinned blowing of air through nostrils curious, flared.
They come, deepened and muscular movements
conjured out of sleep: each small noise and scent
heavy with earth, simple beyond communion,
beyond the stretched-out hand from which they calmly
take corncobs, pulling away as I hold
until the mid-points snap.
They are careful of my fingers,
offering that animal-knowledge,
the respect which is due to strangers;
and in the night, their mares' eyes shine, reflecting stars,
the entire, outer light of the world here.

IN A NET OF BLUE AND GOLD

When the moored boat lifts, for its moment,
out of the water like a small cloud—
this is when I understand.
It floats there, defying the stillness to break,
its white hull doubled on the surface smooth as glass.
A minor miracle, utterly purposeless.
Even the bird on the bow-line takes it in stride,
barely shifting his weight before resuming
whatever musing it is birds do;
and the fish continue their placid, midday
truce with the world, suspended a few feet below.
I catch their gleam, the jeweled, reflecting scales,
small dragons guarding common enough treasure.
And wonder how, bound to each other as we are
in a net of blue and gold,
we fail so often, in such ordinary ways.

INVOCATION

This August night, raccoons,
come to the back door
burnished all summer by salty,
human touch: enter secretly & eat.

Listen, little mask-faced ones,
unstealthy bandits whose tails
are barred with dusk:
listen, gliding green-eyed ones:
I concede you gladly
all this much-handled stuff,
garbage, grain,
the cropped food and cropped heart—
may you gnaw in contentment
through the sleep-hours
on everything left out.

May you find the house
hospitable,
well-used,
stocked with sufficient goods.
I'll settle with your leavings,

as you have settled for mine,
before startling back into darkness
that marks each of us so differently.

TO HEAR THE FALLING WORLD

Only if I move my arm a certain way,
it comes back.
Or the way the light bends in the trees
this time of year,
so a scrap of sorrow, like a bird, lights on the heart.
I carry this in my body, seed
in an unswept corner, husk-encowled and seeming safe.
But they guard me, these small pains,
from growing sure
of myself and perhaps forgetting.

DIALOGUE

A friend says,
"I'm always practicing to be an old woman."
Another answers,
"I see myself young, maybe fourteen."

But when I lean to that mirror
a blackbird wing rises,
dark, flashing red at the shoulder,

and no woman is there
to pin flowers over the place
where her left breast lifts, falls.

RAIN IN MAY

The blackened iron
of the stove
is ticking into coolness
when the first drops
start against the roof.
It is late: the night
has darkened into this
like a fruit—
a sudden
pear-aroma fills the room.

Just before dawn
it comes up harder again,
a white, steady drum of day-rain
caught in the moon's deep pail.
A battered tin-light
overspills ocean and sky,
hill opens to facing hill,
and I wake to a simple longing,
all I want of this ordinary hour,
this ordinary earth
that was long ago married to time:
to hear as a sand crab hears the waves,
loud as a second heart;
to see as a green thing sees the sun,
with the undividing attention of blind love.

JUSTICE WITHOUT PASSION

My neighbor's son, learning piano,
moves his fingers through the passages
a single note at a time, each lasting an equal interval,
each of them loud, distinct,
deliberate as a camel's walk through sand.
For him now, all is dispassion, a simple putting in place;
and so, giving equal weight to each mark in his folded-back book,
bending his head towards the difficult task,
he is like a soldier or a saint: blank-faced, and given wholly
to an obedience he does not need to understand.
He is even-handed, I think to myself,
and so, just. But in what we think of as music
there is no justice, nor in the evasive beauty of this boy,
glimpsed through his window across the lawn,
nor in what he will become, years from now, whatever he will
    become.
For now though, it is the same to him:
right note or wrong, he plays only for playing's sake
through the late afternoon, through stumbling and error,
through children's songs, Brahms, long-rehearsed, steady
    progressions
as he learns the ancient laws—that human action is judgment,
each note struggling with the rest.
That justice lacking passion fails, betrays.

TROMPE L'OEIL

What you understand no longer matters:
the rain beats its steady solo on the roof
and you can hear the saints
assenting, "Get that jazz!" while the old
dropped drumsticks clatter on, unowned.
Or else the sky is empty, blue on blue,
ascending towards an unremitting cold—trompe
l'oeil, all this azure the atmosphere's trick.
You think you can hold on to it,
but erosion cups the garden into being.
Look at the alley there,
between the buildings: how the motes dance down,
slip between gravity and air.
See how the sliding days silt in with seeing, drown.

THE SONG

The tree, cut down this morning,
is already chainsawed and quartered, stripped
of its branches, transported and stacked.
Not an instant too early, its girl slipped away.
She is singing now, a small figure
glimpsed in the surface of the pond.
As the wood, if taken too quickly, will sing
a little in the stove, still remembering her.

SLEEPING IN THE AFTERNOON

The heat-stunned hills at midday
grow gradually quiet,
even the insects' hum lulls deep
within that belled flower, red-throated, cool,
closed eyelids against the light.
Then crossing the serene, dark hips,
the rounded shoulders rubbed smooth
by the south-prevailing wind,
to the muscled, recumbent back
where you ride consenting, as a ship
consents to its mooring when the weather is kind,
the wind easy and full of the scent of desert
and ripening figs. This drifting
can only be wondered at:
perfect and huge, your own chalked thoughts
and history like cupped seeds.
All bannered and streaming with colored flags
that signal the four horizons of unknowing peace—
how you stop then, calm and complete in the snapping sounds,
the rainbowed geometry.

And the telephone's ringing that summons you back
is no more and no less than the prayer-call of a world
that has always pulled you forth with her promises:
everything etched and distinct and all your questions
answered, if only you will choose again,
this once more, to be born,
to carry existence as Atlas carries the earth, continually
and with unchanged diligence, though tricked into it,
though he thought he had escaped.

ARS POETICA

These flat and leathery leaves
of a dry country,
dust on window ledges, grip
of roots in the dirt—
see
how the crone cups us
in parched palms,
blows a little wind into the ear:
garlic, wild rose.

WOMAN IN RED COAT

Some questions cannot be answered.
They become familiar weights in the hand,
round stones pulled from the pocket,
unyielding and cool.
Your fingers travel their surfaces,
lose themselves finally
in the braille of the durable world.
Look out of any window, it's the same—
the yellow leaves, the wintering light.
A truck passes, piled deep in cut wood.
A woman, in a red wool coat,
sees you watching and quickly looks away.

THIS RIPENESS

Thin roads splice field to field
in the early light;
under the trees, many pears
lie opening to the ground.
This ripeness is the landscape I want,
a hand on the kitchen table
passing from sunlight to shadow, warm wood
to cool, and back, behind me the bright jars
ranked on their shelves—harvest
of rutted lanes, too small for naming,
that lead, one to another, through the day.

MUSIC

Why should they please us so,
those impossible runs,

or the knowledge
that the pianist's hand
has spanned an inhuman distance?

That someone years ago conceived
this might be true
and once again it's proved?

Light bends in water,
breaks inside cut glass;
I watched this endlessly as a child.

And now do not know which one
I want more
when sometimes I hear the sound,

sometimes the silence,
and they are equally beautiful
and bare.

AT NIGHT

it is best
to focus your eyes
a little off to one side;
it is better to know things
drained of their color, to fathom
the black horses cropping
at winter grass,
their white jaws that move
in steady rotation, a sweet sound.

And when they file off to shelter
under the trees
you will find the pale circles of snow
pushed aside, earth opening
its single, steadfast gaze:
towards stars ticking by, one by one, overhead,
the given world flaming precisely out of its frame.

HEAT

My mare, when she was in heat,
would travel the fenceline for hours,
wearing the impatience
in her feet into the ground.

Not a stallion for miles, I'd assure her,
give it up.

She'd widen her nostrils,
sieve the wind for news, be moving again,
her underbelly darkening with sweat,
then stop at the gate a moment, wait
to see what I might do.
Oh, I knew
how it was for her, easily
recognized myself in that wide lust:
came to stand in the pasture
just to see it played.
Offered a hand, a bucket of grain—
a minute's distraction from passion
the most I gave.

Then she'd return to what burned her:
the fence, the fence,
so hoping I might see, might let her free.
I'd envy her then,
to be so restlessly sure
of heat, and need, and what it takes
to feed the wanting that we are—

only a gap to open
the width of a mare,
the rest would take care of itself.
Surely, surely I knew that,

who had the power of bucket
and bridle—
she would beseech me, sidle up,
be gone, as life is short.
But desire, desire is long.

2

FOR WHAT BINDS US

DESIRE

For years, the habit of wanting you,
carried like something unnoticed,
lint in a pocket, or manzanita
seed waiting a fire—
you come to me
changed, an old photograph
blurred with motion,
the shutter too slow to keep you the same.
After a while, the light, an old habit
between us, drains off:
simple to meet, to walk towards evening
in a park at the continent's edge;
simple to talk
until conversation drains off,
a newly decanted wine,
and we're left with the sediment dark
at bottom between us,
desire,
simple to say,
and all the decision pours out of my life,
leaving me buoyant, empty, to float
towards your hand.

TO DRINK

I want to gather your darkness
in my hands, to cup it like water
and drink.
I want this in the same way
as I want to touch your cheek—
it is the same—
the way a moth will come
to the bedroom window in late September,
beating and beating its wings against cold glass;
the way a horse will lower
his long head to water, and drink,
and pause to lift his head and look,
and drink again,
taking everything in with the water,
everything.

IN YOUR HANDS

I begin to grow extravagant,
like kudzu,
that rank, green weed
devouring house after house
in the South—
towards midday, the roof tiles
start to throw
a wavering light
back towards the sun,
and roads begin to soften,
darken,
taking your peregrine tongue,
your legs, your eyes,
home to shuttered windows,
to the cool rooms
that invent themselves
slowly into life.

SLEEPING

Here, we are one geography:
every part of us inked on a map
where, across all the blue waters,
continents' edges inexplicably match.

I move closer to you in the dark,
feel the slow heat
that embers you deeper into the night.
Where all fires descend a few hours
into their own slow-dreaming hearts.
Where the ravine hides in its own steepness
no matter how long, how fiercely we love.

SEE HOW THE ROADS ARE STREWN

See how the roads are strewn
white,
as if your hand, traveling my body,
came to be that flock of blossoms,
scent of February in the dark.
See how my hips eclipse your hips,
how the moon, huge as a grain-barge, passes by.
And promises do not hold,
certainties do not hold,
the risen cries fall and fail to hold,
but my body, confusion of crossings, I give you
broadcast, to move with your hand,
where nothing is saved but breaks out in a thousand directions,
armful of wild plum, weeds.

OF GRAVITY & ANGELS

And suddenly, again,
I want the long road of your thigh
under my hand, your well-traveled thigh,
your salt-slicked & come-slicked thigh,
and I want the taste of you, slaking,
under my tongue (that place of riding desire,
my tongue) and I want
all the unnameable, soft, and yielding places,
belly & neck & the place wings would rise from
if we were angels,
and we are, and I want the rising regions of you
shoulder & cock & tongue & breathing &
suddenness of you
opening
all fontanel, all desire, the whole thing beginning
for the first time again, the first,
until I wonder then how is it
we even know which part we are,
even know the ground that lifts us, raucous,
out of ourselves,
as the rising sound of a summer dawn
when all of it joins in.

I HAVE NO USE FOR VIRGINS

I have no use for virgins—
give me the cup
with a chipped lip,
whose handle is glued back on
and whose glaze is dark from use.
Let many men and women
drink from us before
we drink—
I taste their breasts on your breast,
you cover their blaze between my legs.

TONIGHT THE INCALCULABLE STARS

Tonight the incalculable stars
have me thinking of
Catullus and his Lesbia,
who began counting once
and could not stop
until every schoolchild's tongue
pronounced their kisses
interminable,
stumbling through memorized passion
past ancient, jealous crones—
the old arithmetic of love,
got down by heart,
the hard way,
in a foreign tongue, too young.

A DIFFERENT RISING

I reflect, in the bath,
on your penis—
how it floats, lotuslike,
loose-stemmed, a different rising.
And as it hardens, dips:
a long-billed bird, curving for fish.

But mostly we are made
of a heavier stuff,
the slow descent of breast,
foot-arches flattening towards earth,
the hundred ways the body longs for home.
Even those red worlds,
the hybrid dahlias—
despite the bamboo stakes,
the wire,
leaning further groundward with every flower—
with what love or greed or vast indifference
gravity pulls them down.

While in the water bird's throat,
the white, visible pulse of a fish.
Between being and becoming,
turning wildly
as it falls.

TOWARD THE SOLSTICE

9 A.M., already
the day is gathering into heat,
and the hills today are a little less green than they were,
like the flowers closing now into one concentrated whorl,
their color pulled to a tightening heart.

I woke this morning thinking of your lips,
how they lie flat,
almost smiling when you sleep,
and of your hair
that feels much like a child's;
in a room somewhere east of here
you may have turned within that thought,
caught in the cool scent of bleach and hotels,
the white hum of summer night rising towards day.

I have little to offer in this time when nothing lasts,
only that desire
to which you come as to a well.
Even the language tells it:
to satisfy and *sadness* rooted on one stock,
the faithful breathing back towards shadow
of everything that once bent to the sun.

And still, the long slanting days pull us in,
the warmth, the pitch of the hills,
and everything in us wants to give over again—
Only a little further,
a hand's extending, a single word;
the mirage, beautiful, beckons us on.

SURROUNDED BY ALL THE FALLING

After four days of rain
sunlight fills the branches like returning birds,
one of those flocks men believed
they could shoot at forever and never reach the end.
They went fluttering, one by one,
to extinction in seven years.

But this day startles in its sudden gold,
its colored persimmons, rust, and fallen
pine needles blond as a child's hair on the barber's floor;
the sound of his snipping businesslike and crisp.
When loss reaches her, she cannot even cry out,
But where has it gone?
And the sky, so utterly blue it can barely be faced.
It is time to plant bulbs again,
to fork and seed the empty beds into flower.
I turn to feel the sleep-warmth of your hands,
the even breathing that tells me you are close by—
it is still the only story that lets me wake content,
emerge from all the falling of dreams,
the crowded harbor of ships whose riggings
ring like bells,
dance like circus wires.

The girl slides down from the swiveling chair,
her hair combed to new curls.
Soon enough,
I can tell by this day's
windowed, blowsy beauty, it will begin to snow.
She will lie down in it, carefully move
her arms once up, once down

and rise to contemplate quietly, a long time,
the wings she has carved herself out of the cold.

DOPPELGÄNGER

The old knot:
cleave to this,
though faithfulness, all faithfulness,
cuts at the heart
(that wreckage carved out by choice, the heart)
& *cleave this*—
whatever is split
will carry its shadow, that second road,
its yellow leaves falling and falling
in the steep woods of our hundred other lives.

THAT FALLING

You turn towards meteor showers in August,
wishing yourself like that:
bright and burning wholly out.
When feeling finally comes it is
that falling, matter breaking away
from air, the sound
of crickets moving through the grass like fire—
and the strangely twisted metal
in the field that a child finds:
residue, crown.
Then there's the story of the Chinese sage,
in anger and despair, who cut his body away in pieces,
flung them into the lake.
Each one, becoming finned and whole, swims off.

THE MUSIC LIKE WATER

How, on a summer night,
the mysterious few bird notes rise
and break against the dark and stop,
and that music continues, afterward, for a long time;
how you move in me until silence itself is moving
precisely as those few notes,
how they do not stop, the music like water
finding its way;
how what we begin we only think is ours,
how quickly it passes from reach,
some other life throating the air
until it is utterly lovely and changed;
how I am changed by you and change you,
how we willingly hollow our throats for the song,
how the music chains us, but the song—
on a summer night, how it breaks and stops,
how we falter and still the notes rise, beyond us,
how they complete themselves in the silence
and silence completes us, simple as those few notes
that answer the dark on a summer night and fall still.

FOR WHAT BINDS US

There are names for what binds us:
strong forces, weak forces.
Look around, you can see them:
the skin that forms in a half-empty cup,
nails rusting into the places they join,
joints dovetailed on their own weight.
The way things stay so solidly
wherever they've been set down—
and gravity, scientists say, is weak.

And see how the flesh grows back
across a wound, with a great vehemence,
more strong
than the simple, untested surface before.
There's a name for it on horses,
when it comes back darker and raised: proud flesh,

as all flesh
is proud of its wounds, wears them
as honors given out after battle,
small triumphs pinned to the chest—

And when two people have loved each other
see how it is like a
scar between their bodies,
stronger, darker, and proud;
how the black cord makes of them a single fabric
that nothing can tear or mend.

3

THE OTHER EARTH

NOVEMBER, REMEMBERING VOLTAIRE

In the evenings
I scrape my fingernails clean,
hunt through old catalogues for new seed,
oil workboots and shears.
This garden is no metaphor—
more a task that swallows you into itself,
earth using, as always, everything it can.
I lend myself to unpromising winter dirt
with leaf-mold and bulb,
plant into the oncoming cold.
Not that I ever thought
the philosopher meant to be taken literally,
but with no invented God overhead,
I conjure a stubborn faith in rotting
that ripens into soil,
in an old corm that rises steadily each spring:
not symbols, but reassurances,
like a mother's voice at bedtime reading a long-familiar book,
the known words barely listened to,
but joining, for all the nights of a life,
each world to the next.

OSIRIS

They may tell you the god is broken
into a higher life,
but it isn't true:
the one who comes back remains,
even riveted, even pieced-
together in spring,
an always-broken god.
The knots survive in his body,
the clenched-grain scars.
And the iced winter ponds are real:
the children, skating lightly there,
feel a secret shiver
as they cross the blue places
of darkness rising-to-meet,
where the other face of the god
is looking up.

PROTEUS ENTERING WATER

For him, the world was tangential, to be abandoned,
like the line of his body entering water, turning off
to another angle, another life.
From the trees the shore-birds rose steep-winged and grey,
seeing only the widening rings of fish.
Ripples that intersected where he stood, waist-deep in air,
moving off from him changed.
When the birds entered, their wings so closed it was
another being, oiled and sleek, that pursued.
A short time after, each one reappeared with its prize,
assumed the form, once again, of bird. Not knowing what it
    had been.
And he, Proteus, had gone—
taking with him all the unmissed, possible realms,
the golden-clawed beings with their many voices,
the lion-colored light.

ON THE CURRENT EVENTS

The shadows of countries are changing,
like the figures in the dreams of a long sickness.

Argentina, which used to be so full of sunlight
and heroic, whistling pampas cowboys.
Greece, the lovely heifer of curving horns.
Thailand, Palestine, Salvador.

Of course, it is not this constant thing, history,
but ourselves,
like the wooden statue of some sacred figure,
wormed through,

with the bitter aftertaste on the heart
of too much coffee,
any evening,
after too much talk of unimportant things,

when all of it is important:
the cup placed with such a good fit
on its saucer, well and carefully made,
all the still-pieced pieces of our shared consent.

FOR THE WOMEN OF POLAND:
DECEMBER 1981

I think of you standing
at the crossing of two streets,
where even the leaves have turned
accomplices of the cold.
You yield of yourselves
a patience, a hunger,
as other women might, at market,
offer a simpler crop:
robust ears of corn,
potatoes with green-sprouting eyes.
Everywhere there are lines,
people hoping for butter, or freedom,
or meat.
There are cards
with names printed on them
to be sold—cigarettes for flour,
playwrights for engineers.
It is a kind of love, your fingers
grown raw rubbing the wool of your coats,
the bark of these trees;
to touch anything
by now like touching yourself.
And the days draw on inevitably
as those lights of a once-great city
that tell you now stop, now go,
long after you've made up your minds
to stay stubbornly on,
grinding out an old music
on a hand-cranked gramophone
of a heart.

EVENING, LATE FALL

It is not this world, then, to blame, with its red
and blue stars, yellow pears, green apples
that carry a scent which can move you to tears.
The others are not unlike this—
the women stand over sinks with their sleeves pushed back,
thin oxen lean into their yokes,
snow falls with impossible lightness in spring.
How do we bear it, then, to guess sometimes
at their lives across the dark?
How they sing as they run cotton towels across porcelain plates?
How they are innocent?

OCTOBER 20, 1983

On a quiet morning in autumn
I read the ledgers of a war,
as one can any day—
any list biased, dishonest, incomplete,
and still the numbers are kept.
It is true, the papyrus wears thin
after forty centuries.

For the winter garden
roses are pruned and carefully tied,
earth banked up over the roots.
What if after Antigone, the moment of catharsis,
we quarrel in the car going home?
If compassion cannot cure us?
What if we fail?

I look at my hands, my fingernails
still black with chosen labors.
I know that tomorrow I will go out again to mulch,
to bind, to clip, and that no order imposed
is free of guilt.
The line from a Greek chorus:
Sing Sorrow, Sorrow, but Good win out in the end.
But who is measuring, what heart would choose this tune?

ON READING BRECHT

A child packs snow around a bit of stone
and throws it at his brother.
Each recalls this all his life,
the one who threw, and the one who cried out in surprise.
And whatever there is of love between them includes it.

So, too, these words of Brecht's,
who could not forget
what man does to man in the name of art
or country, yet pressed these poems hard,
and threw.

THE ATTEMPT

It is not that they failed to come; they came.
Or that they could not see.
Reaching for us with their arms not much longer than ours,
not whiter, not more pure.
In the mirror of the lake, we were not less beautiful—
Only banked in snow,
like those cities of the far North, to which no roads lead.

THE HUNGRY GHOSTS

The flavors—
apple, cucumber, wine—how they haunt us.
Sting of snow on the tongue, of salt.
Until they make another knowledge, another history,
those strange fruits brought back from the East,
the spices pungent with camel and distant earth.
How in each of us then sails whip and stream with wind
and wooden hulls lower with oranges and sullen, frightened beasts.
And the women calling in markets, across their blanketed tables,
emptying baskets in the first light—how their voices
reach for us like a caress, or a little fire,
whose burning signals to burning across the hills, a smoke-scented
rising, capsicum, myrrh. How we became that heat.
So that now we are neither offering nor offerer nor god: only the
    flame
that, once asked for, cannot be refused.

In Buddhist cosmology, the realm of the Hungry Ghosts
is one of the six possible forms of existence.

ITHACA IN ARMS

Oh, yes, the shuttle
clacks solidly home,
and then the real work's begun:
the stealthy, lavish unraveling,
wool soft & bent between fingers: altered,
kinked.

You learn to take a life apart, to wait.
These are the richest hours,
silence and darkness,
the clattering quelled.
What's loomed on this lasts well:
fine swords unbuckled,
ambition, doubt
laid down with lamb shanks for the dogs.

Give the best meat away:
so far will hospitality extend.
For the rest, do without:
doing without doing, the years supplant themselves,
suitors gone bored while waiting for your hand.
And so, time can be stopped after all—
only the future foreshortened,
a trick of perspective,
like the wool-skein growing smaller every day.

IN THAT WORLD, THE ANGELS WEAR FINS

In that world, the angels wear fins.
Red hulls pass over like clouds, their shadows
angling down between ropes of sun.
When women who have dived there return,
they do not speak of oysters or pearls.
Shaking their heads they say, "There is nothing."
They say, "We must look somewhere else,"
and twist their black hair in the world of men,
and wade heavily through the grass-scented air.
From this they know loss like salt:
how without it, the tongue grows stubborn and dull,
tastes nothing.
But the wild flavor, the sea, how it moves in them,
hip and thigh—a soundless current, kicking
downward the rest of their lives.

UKIYO-E

The blues' plunge,
the oranges edging towards dun
catch the eye—a certain perspective,
singular,
a certain weathering of inks.

I think of the Floating World
as the prints themselves,
not the district where they sold:
landscapes, actors, and geisha unmoored,
the paper flimsy and cheap,
betraying the subjects' own quickness
to change:
the sumo wrestler's fierce eye will grow mild,
his black hair grey,
while passing from hand to hand for a hundred years
the sky of Edo deepens,
readies itself for the first pale stars
that will not come.

RECALLING A SUNG DYNASTY LANDSCAPE

Palest wash of stone-rubbed ink
leaves open the moon: unpainted circle,
how does it raise so much light?
Below, the mountains
lose themselves in dreaming
a single, thatch-roofed hut.
Not that the hut lends meaning
to the mountains or the moon—
it is a place to rest the eye after much traveling,
is all.
And the heart, unscrolled,
is comforted by such small things:
a cup of green tea rescues us, grows deep and large,
a lake.

COOK

Each night you come home with five continents on your hands:
garlic, olive oil, saffron, anise, coriander, tea,
your fingernails blackened with marjoram and thyme.
Sometimes the zucchini's flesh seems like a fish-steak,
cut into neat filets, or the salt-rubbed eggplant
yields not bitter water, but dark mystery.
You cut everything to bits.
No core, no kernel, no seed is sacred: you cut
onions for hours and do not cry,
cut them to thin transparencies, the red ones
spreading before you like fallen flowers;
you cut scallions from white to green, you cut
radishes, apples, broccoli, you cut oranges, watercress,
romaine, you cut your fingers, you cut and cut
beyond the heart of things, where
nothing remains, and you cut that too, scoring coup
on the butcherblock, leaving your mark,
when you go
your feet are as pounded as brioche dough.

RESTRINGING THE BEADS

One by one
they fall into place
on silk thread,
with the small, light click
of the lid of a box: a perfect fit.
108 rounded bones,
the lives of the monks
rejoin one another,
a broken-off conversation resumes,
in the refectory
their chopsticks
play on lacquered bowls.

POMEGRANATES

Under
a thin coat of dust
dull globes
of pomegranates
ripen.

No easy fruit,
these sweet-seeded
leatherskinned
puckering
moons
that clench
& pull the brushwood
closer to ground—

Wild branches
interweave
into a thickening idiom
of wood:

muttered polysyllabic of twig,
guttural patois
of leaf
in a green-belled dusk,
and the vowels, slurred,
hanging
in drunken heat.

Yes, they say (that sweetness
in the mouth mixing with pith,
a difficult promise
made once to a dark King),
yes, I will return everything.

A STORY

A woman tells me
the story of a small wild bird,
beautiful on her window sill, dead three days.
How her daughter came suddenly running,
"It's moving, Mommy, he's alive."
And when she went, it was.
The emerald wing-feathers stirred, the throat
seemed to beat again with pulse.
Closer then, she saw how the true life lifted
under the wings. Turned her face
so her daughter would not see, though she would see.

NEEDLES OF PINE, OF MORNING

By this morning, the color has gone from the gold
of child's hair to yellow, stalled straw, to the dun of dry soil.

Still dropping, pine needles pass the window like snow:
things do not stop simply because we have had enough.

And again the newspaper knocks the door, its flung weight
announcing the unwakened world. Over coffee I try to imagine

the stories and fail: the words remain simple, work on the day
unseen as the crooked fingers of wind in the trees.

Still, my lungs lift their habitual cartons of air.
And the ones whose lives I uncrease and turn,

spread out over this white table—I know little of them
but that children, if possible, are fed, the young men

and young women must look at one another, and that it is hard.
And hard too to live in this place where even the best, the
    luckiest,

lose everything if not today then tomorrow or next year
and still we have not found out how to be kind.

What falls, we think, is always on the other side
of the glass, the other side of the world,

and the last fear, helplessness,
covers our eyes like two coins until we cannot see

how the black water rocks beneath us,
how the ferryman, expressionless, holds out his hand.

TAMARA STANDS IN STRAW

and dreams her long-necked, sweet-grass reveries,
and shifts her weight in the patient way
of horses in the cold.
She will be a long time in this stall,
through the entire season of grass
she will have alfalfa, timothy,
an eight-foot, spare enclosure keeping her dry
on hooves held closed with polymer and wire.
This tall barn covers her strangely,
a mare who's never been kept in;
a worn-out structure roofed with tin,
it magnifies the rain.
I am to stay with her for several hours,
to keep her on her feet till the plastic sets.
The stable-owner sends a thermos of tea
and I drink slowly,
taking in its heat
in the faint warmth of the barn;
while the mare dreams and wakes and drinks
and returns to her hay and then her dreaming,
while darkness tightens to the single shape of horse
and night sounds of iron scud against concrete
through all the layered softnesses of straw.

THE OTHER EARTH

At first we embrace trees.
Lie with the swan, the bull, become stars.
Blackbirds form bridges across the sky:
we pass, lightly placing our feet.
The god enters our rooms in a shower of gold.
Into the intricate maze a white thread,
a woman, a fish come to guide our way out.
Docile as horses, we go.

When the plain world comes,
with its explanations
smooth and cool as a marble statue's skin,
we go, rising out of the dark.
Being careless and proud, we look back
towards the other earth:
how it wavers and goes out,
like a girl with an errand to do in another room.

4

THE PATTERN THAT CONNECTS

IN SMOOTH WATER THE MOUNTAINS SUSPEND THEMSELVES

Here, where shallows and hillside
echo each other
so perfectly, who is to say
what is water, what sky,
or what perfection it is that arches
a squirrel's grey body
from oak tree to pine, thirty feet in the air?
He does not think of himself
as one of the many possible angels
plucked from the blue of this lake,
as the one that chose to manifest, just now.
To him, it is no surprise when he crosses
the dim, suspended fluttering of a fish
mid-way in his climb
up the vertical trunk of the world.
He is like one of those ancient creatures
found on cathedral walls,
lion-mouthed, vulture-clawed, with bulging eyes—
how calmly they survey the doors and windows,
what enters, what departs.
No human passage concerns them,
compared to the cool weight of stone,
to the beings whose size those enormous openings fit;
and we, in turn, barely glance towards
their bodied faith sluiced over with rain,
bearded in ice, as we pass beneath.
So the wind-roughened fur of the squirrel brushes
against the belly of the big brown
and their doubles,
perfectly camouflaged above, below,
know nothing of that meeting, its cold, quick touch.
And we, who quarry the earth for silver and granite
with any step,
do not feel the green clouds of treetops, green clouds of weeds—
how they rest like folded wings in the clear water,
patient, waiting, having borne us this far.

IT IS EASY TO BE FASCINATED
WITH DEATH

It is easy to be fascinated with death.
We pretend to prepare,
trying on the oversized high heels,
the string of pearls,
the perfumed throw of another life.
Yet trust we are not truly going to dinner:
our hands—we claim—too small,
too clumsy to properly lift the long-stemmed glass.

AGAINST LOSS

For years I hoped
the stars splashed on blackness
would wrestle themselves into shapes;
envied Scheherazade
dragging desire
like a fish-hook through the dark.

For wasn't the point
that stories, like love,
are spelled out on the skin against loss?

> *A man was left a widower with one daughter . . .*
> *Once, it is told, there was a King . . .*
> *A flock of sheep was standing in a field . . .*

When in Italy, and sixteen,
I threw my coins in with the rest,
wasn't I wanting
that gesture to pull me down
to a world with others,
where everything shines?

And nights when the windows
are shut against night,
isn't it just like lacquer sprinkled with gold,
the way an old loneliness follows you
into sleep and the stories come?

THE SPEED WITH WHICH BLUE
NEEDLES MOVE

As I walk through the daylight
something closes behind me.
I look back and all is as it was:
leaf-shadows dapple the grass,
a grey squirrel runs up the side of a tree,
a truck engine grinds, on a distant road,
shifting gears.
I turn again, walk forward,
and the small pebble rings continue to widen
and flatten into the general water.
I think of my grandmother then, at her work;
take confidence
from the speed with which blue needles move.
After a while she looks up
and names it for me, *each year the day you will die
is hiding among the rest*—
and gives her silent, dead blessing
to the cable-pattern that knots me to this world.

THE PATTERN THAT CONNECTS

Tonight, as you touched my face,
I thought of Gregory's death:
how knowing perhaps that it would please you,
though he had not shaved for weeks,
he asked you to shave him that day.
It is a thing, I realize now,
that neither his wife nor daughter could do;
and I imagine your fingers suddenly less sure,
moving in ways known until then
only from within.
But in your hands' slow remembering
you shaved him as your father had once shaved you,
with large-knuckled, inexpressible joy.
One man can give another so little:
not courage, not time.
The weight of his head for those moments
held in your hand, and then not.
The melody that carries a children's rhyme
through centuries, though the meaning of the words is lost.

COMPLETING THE WEAVE

for M. T.

A woman labors over the stories as over a needlepoint,
each stitch crossed back on itself.
Here, she says to her children, I have put your names,
in a blue the color of china plates,
and here your grandfather knots closed the roof
of the house he made in the Bronx.

She picks a thread also for strength,
one that will hold the tightening pull of the long dead—
they shake white-bearded heads,
mumble the old-country words she understood then,
move cloth-bound hands with fingers missing
over icy piles of fish;
and blink against the being-light of being again called in.

It is careful work; she bends
in the yellow reach of the one lamp burning in the room
and holds the rough scrim a long time between each use.
It is the work of a woman listening
to the life of a village where she never lived—in the way
her fingers curve to grip the needed brightness of needle,
in the way her lips know, even now,
the taste of eastern Europe on her tongue, whispering
past the shape of her past
into the ones that will be:
forgetful one, remember,
in the unbraided days of your life,
these syllables, these crude-drawn forms, these colors
spell God's only name you will know.

A CONTINUOUS EMBROIDERY

1.

The sky's blue deepens to meet
the darkness of trees.
In the window
an old woman's face
looks at me, yellow in the yellow light.
I can see the grain, the winnowing, the chaff
cupped in her hands—
an indiscriminate harvest,
years of shadows settling in like birds.

2.

What is it to look at your hands
and see the veins, at last, completely emerge?
To feel your body's surface erode?
In the quiet nights, all the stark lace-work
starts to come undone,
the fine nerve-net releases its music
gently into the dark.

3.

I asked my grandmother about this
but she told me lies,
stories she'd heard from her own grandmother,
re-worked.
I asked my grandmother again
and she called me by her dead sister's name—
May, she murmured, May.

TOWARD THE INFINITE

You might take it for a given:
how numbers climb
first quickly,
then more slowly toward the infinite,
the way an aging man climbs stairs
first with a hand to the banister,
then pausing between landings,
then not at all.

Or the desert fathers
hunting their God from the beehived caves—
how hunger brought him closer,
lessened the distance
between eye and star,
as light became only an absence
of the long familiar dark.

You near it in circles, the way
a dog circles his sleep before lying down:
the ascetics die with their gnosis
concealed among them, sifted, particular sand.
The man moves to a ground-floor flat and brews his tea,
the numbers continue in lengthy approach.
And your eye for a moment settles
on the breast of a strange girl;
you know her then entirely
before she passes out of view.

WITH SINGING AND BANNERS

Demosthenes, a wise man, filled his mouth
with pebbles before speaking;
and a stream which has run ten feet over rocks
is clear, they say, and safe to drink.
Yet still we forget what is owed our failures—
blessings, to praise the stumbled on stone.
And forget what we once knew, how to properly greet
old enemies, for whose sake we practice and parry,
become strong:
with singing and banners, with gladness.

AUTUMN QUINCE

How sad they are,
the promises we never return to.
They stay in our mouths,
roughen the tongue, lead lives of their own.
Houses built and unwittingly lived in;
a succession of milk bottles brought to the door
every morning and taken inside.

And which one is real?
The music in the composer's ear
or the lapsed piece the orchestra plays?
The world is a blurred version of itself—
marred, lovely, and flawed.
It is enough.

CHILDHOOD, HORSES, RAIN

Again rain:
and the world like a fish held
under running water while the knife-blade
smooths the skin of scales.
Its twin eyes open, watching
not-death, not-life.
We shed our wild selves like this,
fearlessly, as water sheds its smoothness under wind,
and the image breaks, the white house, the apple trees,
the horses quivering with late summer flies as they graze,
the hundred wings brushing the lake of their backs.
Or the dog, who, seeing I will not open the door,
lies down at last to sleep: how, in her dream,
she chases down birds and barks softly.
How later the door will open, and she
in all her black and white ecstasy will burst through
to the scent of damp earth, return shaking rain from her
like seeds to the kitchen floor.
It is late and the dishes are finished, put away.
I towel her dry, she offers her feet up easily, as a horse
from long practice eases the farrier's work:
stands patiently at the hiss of hot iron dipped briefly
into a pail, cooled now and shaped to this one
curve of hoof, pared not quite to the quick;
and the swift blows with their stopped-bell ring.
As we learn to stand, for this world.

LULLABYE

n.: 1. a song to quiet children or to lull
them to sleep; a cradlesong.   2. music for this.
3. good night or good-by; a farewell

for D. M. (1890–1985)

Always there is desire,
only the shape
of what is desired shifts,
each love giving way to another,
from the first sound
of heartbeat inconceivably there,
and on

into the face that rises like a moon
    beyond world's edge;
into the milk that teaches
    earliest meaning, hunger;
into the tumbling of breast, of belly heat,
    of hands, that encourage the body
    to meaning of its own;
into the close-tucked blankets, nascent trust
    that existence will hold through the night;
into the dangled colors, first temptation,
    that come and go;
into the song that wanders beyond knowing
    out of lips;
into the climbing bafflement of change;
into the first power,
    to call forth;
into the second power,
    to move;
into the third power,
into the loneliness of self.

And now, desire fully mounted,
the branch full-laden with flower,

white hands of strangers start to summon
an awkward, ground-risen heat,
knowledge takes root in the body daily more sure,
it cries out and cries out again in startled awe—

Until, when the whole music is breaking
full-throated into the ears,
the next desire begins to whisper
into the stateliness of bones, a pull,
into the steadiness of blood, a weight,

and flavors of early apples appear on the tongue,
feet come to travel the ground more slowly again,
the map of the face grows detailed, a country known,

and the new love comes,
if the heart
will open enough, will let enough go to make room:

love of the structure of things,
    bare branches of trees;
love of the overly large, the poorly made,
    the somehow wrong;
love of the golden net,
    the promises and guile of words;
love of the strength
    that is passing from the legs;
love of the colors
    daily leaving the eyes;
love of the delicacy
    that abandons the wrists;
love of all powers
    that diminish out of the body,
    calling farewell

to the ears that forget to listen,
to the nerve-ends fraying with use,
to the breathing that retrenches into itself,
to the beautiful skin grown tired of dividing the earth
into ours, not ours,
as we tire too, of holding separate,
and love of self that was once so clear
grows suddenly simple, widens,
as a mother's hand smoothing a sheet,
as water that broadens and flattens,
taking the shape of the darkened, still-reflecting world.

ABOUT THE AUTHOR

Jane Hirshfield's first book, *Alaya,* received the Quarterly Review of Literature Prize in 1982. In 1986, *Of Gravity & Angels* received the Joseph Henry Jackson Award from the San Francisco Foundation for a book in progress; in 1989, it was awarded the Commonwealth Club Poetry Medal. Hirshfield's third book, *The October Palace,* published in 1994, received the Bay Area Book Reviewers Award, the Commonwealth Club Poetry Medal, and the Poetry Center Book Award. She has also edited and co-translated *The Ink Dark Moon: Poems by Komachi and Shikibu, Women of the Ancient Court of Japan* (1988), and edited *Women in Praise of the Sacred: 43 Centuries of Spiritual Poetry by Women* (1994). Hirshfield's other honors include a Guggenheim Fellowship, a Rockefeller Foundation Bellagio Fellowship, Columbia University's Translation Center Award, and a Pushcart Prize. She has taught at the University of Califorinia at Berkeley and the University of San Francisco, and lives in Mill Valley, California.

LIBRARY OF CONGRESS CATALOGING-IN-PUBLICATION DATA

Hirschfield, Jane, 1953–
  Of gravity & angels / Jane Hirshfield.—1st ed.
    p.   cm.
  ISBN 0-8195-2136-1   ISBN 0-8195-1138-2 (pbk.)
  I. Title. II. Title: Of gravity & angels.
PS3558.I69403   1988   87-21184
811'.54—dc19